CARAVAGGIO

With an introduction & notes by Trewin Copplestone

MASTERPIECES IN COLOUR · BATCHWORTH PRESS LONDON

BP

Front Cover   *c. 1596   Oil on canvas   37¹/₂ × 33¹/₂ inches   Uffizi, Florence*

Bacchus

This painting was rediscovered in 1916 in the Uffizi store-room
and was first thought to be a copy of Caravaggio, but its quality
soon convinced authorities that it was an original.
It has been suggested that it is the painting described by Baglione
as having been done with great care (*con diligènza*), but there is
some doubt of this, since the important basket of fruit in the
foreground is not mentioned by him.
This Bacchus, the god of wine, is not the pleasure-loving
sybarite that one sees in most representations, supported
or surrounded by his followers in various stages
of drunken ecstasy. He is here a young private sensualist who offers
the viewer a choice of connoisseurs' wine in a delicate hand.
There is about him an air of Roman vulgarity, and one feels that
he is some young boy masquerading in a fancy dress that he has
neither the wit nor the understanding to carry.
The quality of the painting of the still-life is somewhat at variance
with the figure itself, the drawing of which is, in places, weak—as,
for example, the hand holding the glass and the foreshortening
of the arm. The handling of the perspective, which pushes the figure
to the picture plane, invites the participation of the viewer
and seems to suggest his own inadequacy before temptation.
There are reminders of other painters in this work, and if the list
given by Berenson in his biography seems excessive there is an
obvious association with Velasquez' *Topers* (*Los Borrachos*), with Ingres
in the handling of drapery, and with Manet in the flat lighting.

INTRODUCTION

The genius overtaken by an early death is a figure familiar in the history of
European culture; and each is a recurring tragedy for imaginative speculation.
In Britain he is usually a writer, a Marlowe, Shelley, Keats, Byron or, more
recently, a Rupert Brooke or Dylan Thomas. In France and Italy, more frequently he is a painter, a Watteau, Géricault, Van Gogh, Seurat, Masaccio, Giorgione,
Raphael, Correggio, Parmigianino—the list is extensive. Not the least tragic in
life and death alike, not less important but less well known, was the Lombard
painter, Michelangelo Merisi, known as Caravaggio; and rarely can such genius
have invited its early death through so anarchic and irresponsible a life.

'Whom the gods love die young,' they say, but it must have been a strange and *Caravaggio's personality*
capricious love they had for Caravaggio. Hardly lovable by any normal under-
standing and severely handled by what seems an adverse fate, he spent his fiery,
irresponsible, energetic life in destroying through his behaviour the admiration his
talent aroused. His contemporaries agree on this as on nothing else. Baglione, who
brought a libel action against him, was his first biographer and had this to say of
him: '(Caravaggio)... was a satirical and haughty man, he would often speak badly of
all painters of the past and present, no matter how distinguished they were, because
he thought that he alone had surpassed all the other men of his profession. However
some people consider him to have been the very ruination of painting... Because
of the excessive ardour of his spirits, (Caravaggio) was a little dissolute and he seemed
to look for the occasion to break his neck or even to risk the lives of others. He
spent much time in the company of others who, like himself, were quarrelsome by
nature.' Bellori, another biographer, credits him with 'a turbulent and contentious
nature.' Mancini says he was extravagant—we would say dissolute—and thus short-
ened his life by at least ten years. The Dutch writer Van Mander says: '... he
does not pursue his studies steadfastly, so that after a fortnight's work he will
swagger about for a month or two with his sword at his side and a servant following
him, from one tavern to another, always ready to brawl or argue, and most awk-
ward to get along with.' The list could be extended, and Professor Wittkower has
recently described him as 'perhaps the most consistent Bohemian'.

But genius cannot be equated with moral stature, and this unpleasant man was
a great painter. So important in fact is his work that its influence can be traced
in the subsequent art of most countries of Europe. Important as it is, however,
inevitably something of his character appears in his work, which diminishes its
charm while revealing its power. Caravaggio is undoubtedly a difficult painter to
love in both life and work.

What he wished to bring to painting was an uncompromising attitude to life, *Uncompromising attitude to his art*
devoid of all hypocrisy: a realism in the treatment of subject matter in opposition
to what he thought to be the over-bred and over-mannered culture of his day. We
shall return later to an examination of his success in this respect, but perhaps it
should be mentioned here that this deliberately anti-cultural attitude could, and
in Caravaggio's case did, lead to a pictorial vulgarity and a fleshy sensuality.

He was born Michelangelo Merisi, on September 28th, 1573, in Caravaggio, the *Early life and influences*
small town near Bergamo from which he derives the name by which he is usually
known. Bergamo lies between Milan and Brescia, in the Alpine foothills, near Lake
Como, and thus it was close to the two great traditions in Italian art, the Tuscan
and the Venetian. Both influences are present in Caravaggio's art; particularly is
he known to have admired Giorgione and the late Venetians. Federico Zuccari
went so far in a comment on the *Calling of St Matthew* (Plate 6) as to call it 'nothing
but an idea of Giorgione'. The influence may be partly attributable to Caravaggio's
first master, Simone Peterzano, a mediocre painter who came from the Venetian
area and worked in Milan.

The known facts of Caravaggio's life are scanty, particularly in the earlier years, *Apprenticeship to Peterzano*
but it is apparent from surviving documents that he was apprenticed to Peterzano
in 1584, with his elder brother acting as guardian. This suggests that his father,
architect or master of works to the Marchese of Caravaggio, had previously died.
We have no knowledge of Caravaggio's mother.

It may be assumed that he finished his apprenticeship with Peterzano, although
this would have been an unusually disciplined act on his part, and that he left in
1588. It is not known whether he stayed in Milan for a while, went straight to
Rome, or made a short trip to Venice. It would be of great interest if more details
of his activities after leaving Peterzano were known, for he was only fifteen at the

completion of his apprenticeship and had painted his *Boy with Fruit* (Plate 2) and *Boy with a Basket of Fruit* (Plate 3) before he was twenty, and his development must have been rapid during these years of obscurity. There is no direct evidence for the assumption but a short stay in Venice is not improbable. All that is certain is that he was next heard of in Rome. Authorities differ as to the date of his arrival in the Eternal City, but it was probably around 1590.

The early years in Rome

He appears to have lived in extreme poverty for some time after his arrival, and both Bellori and Baglione say that he worked for a Sicilian painter called Lorenzo —all accounts indicate that Lorenzo was a wretched hack who could have had nothing but a depressing effect on Caravaggio. He is also said to have been the assistant for six months of a certain Pandolfo Pucci, working on religious paintings. During this time he spent a period in the Hospital for the Poor in Santa Maria della Consolazione, recovering from an attack of malaria. While there he did some painting for the Prior as the only form of payment open to him, which the Prior is supposed to have sent to Seville or Sicily. The distinction is of some significance, for if the paintings were sent to Seville this could account for his early influence upon Velasquez, at that time a young man in the town; some recent support for Seville has been provided by the discovery of Spanish connections in the Prior's family. The painting *Boy with Fruit* has been claimed as a self-portrait done while he was recuperating from this illness.

In 1591, Caravaggio probably spent some months working as an apprentice assistant in the studio of Giuseppe Cesari, later known as the Cavaliere d'Arpino, only five years older than Caravaggio but already making a name for himself. It seems that d'Arpino set him to paint flower and fruit pieces and it is possible that *Bacchus* (Plate 1) and *Boy with Fruit* were done as exercises on his own account while he was working for d'Arpino. The evidence is strengthened by the fact that these paintings were in d'Arpino's possession when his goods were sequestered for non-payment by the tax authorities in 1607.

Caravaggio, chafing under the restraint of doing hack work for a painter only five years his senior—to a youth of his temperament this was almost a personal slight—set up on his own but was unsuccessful and was soon in the greatest poverty. Eventually, however, helped by other painters, he was introduced to Cardinal del Monte, who took him into his house, secured work for him and thus became his first important patron. Del Monte was a man of great position, an intimate of the Pope, with considerable influence, and it was through him that Caravaggio was really launched on his career. His support brought Caravaggio his first great commission, in the Contarelli Chapel in the Church of San Luigi dei Francesi in Rome.

The Contarelli Chapel

The decoration of this chapel had begun in 1592, and d'Arpino had painted only the ceiling panels when a prolonged lawsuit over the decoration caused the chapel to be boarded up for five years. In 1597, redecoration was begun and Cardinal del Monte was one of a committee set up to investigate the situation. They arranged that a sculptured group, which was to have been the altar-piece, should be replaced by a painting of *St Matthew and the Angel*, by Caravaggio, who was also given a commission for two large side-paintings, or laterals, *The Calling of St Matthew* and *The Martyrdom of St Matthew* (Plates 6 and 7). Caravaggio's first *St Matthew and the Angel* was rejected; it seems to have pleased no one and it did not fit its architectural setting. The situation was saved by a great admirer of Caravaggio, the Marchese Giustiniani, who not only bought the rejected painting but offered to pay for the replacement which was accepted and placed in the position it still holds above the altar. The first painting was eventually, in 1815, purchased by the Kaiser Friedrich Museum in Berlin, where it is supposed to have been destroyed by fire in 1944.

Difficulties with the police

In 1600, Caravaggio was still living in the house of Cardinal del Monte, and while there he made his first of many appearances in police records. It frequently happens that, once a man impatient of authority gets into trouble he seems unable to keep out of it and also develops a strong antipathy to any representative of authority. This was certainly the case with Caravaggio, who was at all times intolerant of any intrusion upon what he considered his rights and dignities. On one occasion in Rome he was stopped for his permit to carry a sword. Although he actually had one, he said to the officer, 'You and the others with you can shove off,' which, not surprisingly, landed him in jail. On another occasion a certain Pietro, in a police report, said: 'I was having dinner in the Tavern of the Blackamoor. On the other side of the room there was Michelangelo da Caravaggio, the painter. I heard him ask whether the artichokes were done in oil or butter, they being all in one plate. The waiter said "I don't know," and picked up one and put it to his nose. Michelangelo took it amiss, sprang to his feet in rage, and said, "If I am not mistaken, you damned cuckold, you think you are serving some bum," and he seized the plate with the artichokes on it and threw it at the waiter's face. I did not see the painter grasp his sword to threaten the waiter.' Examples of these petty offences were numerous, and some of his involvements were far more serious.

The most catastrophic in its eventual effect was the death of a young man, Ranuccio Tomassoni, with whom he had been playing racquets. During a dispute, probably over the score, Tomassoni was stabbed in the groin by Caravaggio and died. Caravaggio himself was wounded and fled from the scene. While still recuperating in bed, Caravaggio was questioned by the Clerk of the Court and claimed with supreme effrontery and improbability that he was alone at the time and had slipped and fallen on his sword, which accounted for the wound on the back of his neck. Naturally he was not believed and, despite the efforts of his influential friends, was banished from Rome.

This incident occurred in 1606, and before this he had completed a number of his important works, of which we illustrate the unique *Basket of Fruit* (Plate 5), the *Cupid Victorious* (Plate 8), a curious work done for the Marchese Giustiniani, the sombre *David with the Head of Goliath* (Plate 11), and the extraordinary and revealing *Conversion of St Paul* (Plate 9). This last was one of two paintings commissioned from Caravaggio for the Cerasi Chapel in the Church of Santa Maria del Popolo, the other being a *Martyrdom of St Peter*. The first versions of both these paintings were refused, but the second are still in place.

Caravaggio was a quick and industrious painter and even in his flight managed to complete some work. While at Paliano near Palestrina, sheltering with Don Marzio Colonna, he painted the *Supper at Emmaus* (Plate 10), which was immediately sent to Rome and sold to the Marchese Patrizi, in whose family it remained until bought by the Brera Gallery in 1939.

Eventually he arrived in Naples where his friends had sent his painting materials. He recommenced work on the unfinished commissions he had received before he left Rome.

The Neapolitan period

Rome, however, did not immediately forget him. His painting of the *Death of the Virgin* was publicly exhibited in 1607, drawing large crowds and extremely varied critical comments. It served as a means of propagating Caravaggio's art, and Northern artists like Honthorst and Vouet, both in Rome at the time, may well have seen it. The qualities of the painting were extolled by Rubens, who was also in Rome, and he recommended its purchase to the Duke of Mantua.

The great interest this painting aroused stemmed from the treatment that Caravaggio gave this, to the Roman Church, central subject. The painting is also particularly revealing of his pictorial philosophy. The model that he used for the Virgin was a well-known prostitute, an acquaintance of his, whose bloated, drowned body had been fished from the Tiber. His desire for realism demanded a real body, and his concern was more with the outward aspect of death than with the spiritual significance of the Mother of Jesus. He probably did not think of the shock that his unconventional choice of model might cause—if he did he is likely to have cocked a deliberate snook of wry defiance at conventional attitudes.

In the same year, 1607, Caravaggio made another move—from Naples to Malta. This appeared full of promise and Caravaggio's success seemed assured. But, of course, with Caravaggio success could not last. The reason for his decision to move is not known. It may have been the promise of a knighthood; perhaps it was the distance from his many creditors and enemies; perhaps it was to escape the consequences of some crime committed in Naples which has so far not come to light. In any case he was certainly welcomed with great favour by the Grand Master of the Order of the Knights of St John, Alof de Wignacourt. He painted two portraits of this autocratic, powerful man, one of which is lost, the other now in the Louvre.

Visit to Malta

Probably the most important work he painted in Malta is the deeply impressive *Beheading of John the Baptist* (Plate 12), one of his greatest works, which, with the painting of St Jerome done at the same time, is still in the Cathedral at Valletta.

In 1608, Caravaggio was received into the Order of Malta as a token of the esteem in which the Grand Master then held him, and he was given various presents, including two Turkish slaves and a gold chain. With his talent for trouble only two or three months later, in the autumn of the same year, he quarrelled with one of his superiors in the Order. He was pitched into jail—a familiar experience for him—and with his usual enterprise he escaped over the prison wall and fled to Syracuse. The Grand Master, not a man of notable tolerance and quick to resent any affront to his dignity, became Caravaggio's implacable enemy, deprived him of his knighthood and sent his agents in pursuit of the irresponsible, ungrateful painter.

Flight and pursuit

Caravaggio, fearful of the consequences of his actions in Malta, did not stay long in Syracuse, although, with his usual ferocious energy, he managed to complete a large painting of the *Martyrdom of St Lucy* for the city fathers.

Probably early in 1609, he left Syracuse for Messina, where he painted a *Resurrection of Lazarus* and a *Nativity*. From Messina, in the summer of 1609, he went to Palermo where, again aware of the pursuit of Wignacourt's men, he stayed only long enough to paint a second *Nativity* before returning to Naples.

Here, on October 24th, the servants of Wignacourt appear to have caught up with him and, according to Bellori, he was attacked in some dark doorway in a sordid part of Naples by a gang of armed men and was so badly wounded about the face that it was said he was scarcely recognisable. In the 'bitterest pain' he boarded a ship for Rome. Probably the cut-throats thought that they had killed him, for a report reached Rome that he was dead.

He had set out for Rome because some of his influential friends had been working for the reprieve of his banishment and they had written suggesting that he come nearer to the scene. Even he had not the temerity to enter Papal territory while still under banishment, and he disembarked with his belongings at Porto Ercole which, being Spanish territory, was not forbidden to him. Before he left Naples, apparently in the fruitless hope of placating the Grand Master, he sent a *Salome with the Head of St John* to Malta.

Death at Porto Ercole

By one of those strokes of misfortune that fate seems always to have reserved for Caravaggio, he was arrested in Porto Ercole for a crime he had, for once, not committed, and before the error was rectified and he was released, the ship carrying his belongings had sailed—or so he believed, and in his fury he chased the ship along the coast under a blazing sun. Actually, his possessions were stored in the Customs House nearby, having been impounded, but this he never discovered, for the heat, combined with his weakened, wounded condition, induced a fever from which, uncared for, on July 18th, 1610, he died.

It was an ironic stroke, in keeping with his life, that three days after his death his pardon came through. It must have been signed about the time he died.

It is more than surprising that so tragic, unsettled a life should have produced an art of such great importance. Although he had only the same short life, Raphael, loved by all who knew him, courted and cosseted in Rome, with continuous patronage and large commissions, had the opportunity for an extensive influence. Caravaggio, a fugitive most of his working life, with a temperament which made him his own worst enemy, could hardly have been expected to achieve anything of lasting effect. And yet he initiated a new and broad stream of European painting. Such an achievement is rare with any painter. With Caravaggio it seems nothing short of miraculous.

Significance of Caravaggio's influence

What was so stimulating and original in his work, and why was its influence so great? To answer this question some understanding of the course of sixteenth-century painting in Italy, and particularly in Rome, is necessary.

From the beginning of the fifteenth century, the Renaissance in the great cultural centres of Italy—Florence, Venice and Rome—had, with its emphasis on human accomplishment and understanding, encouraged the painter and sculptor towards a more accurate presentation of the appearance of the visible. Problems which had not concerned the earlier painters, whose ideas were directed towards a Christian symbolism, seemed very important to the Renaissance artist. To achieve his aims in representation, he required a knowledge of and competence in perspective, aerial and linear, anatomy, the use of light and shade, the effect of light on colour, the dramatic expression of human relationships, proportion and all the minor technical difficulties inherent in drawing. It took the whole of the talent in Italy during the century to acquire this, but by the beginning of the sixteenth century most of the seen problems were overcome and an art which thought to bear closely upon its classical model was achieved in the work of the greatest masters of the High Renaissance, above all in Raphael. The classical model also demanded a knowledge of Greek and Roman mythology and an interpretation of the various classical writers. While the works of such artists as Raphael, Botticelli and Correggio were obviously a more accomplished presentation of the visible world than earlier painters had achieved, they were also an interpretation of classical writers and their Renaissance followers such as Pico della Mirandola and Giordano Bruno.

Caravaggio and Mannerism

This experience and competence gained, the restless spirit of the artist sought more; he became introspective and self-conscious, sophisticated and dissatisfied. He turned away from the classical model of harmony, perfection and idealisation to a form of painting which has come to be known as Mannerism. This was current in Italy from the middle of the fifteenth century to the 1580's, and its influence was pervasive. The origin of the term Mannerism is found in the Italian word *maniera* which meant, literally, 'made by hand'. Gradually it became synonymous with 'mode,' with 'personal style' and eventually 'personal manner'—although the association with mere handwork, with pre-ordered construction, remained. It is in these later associations that the term is now usually applied. The artists associated with it are not as well known as their predecessors, although the most important, Parmigianino, Bronzino, Primaticcio and others, are represented widely in galleries.

Mannerism lasted in endless variations for about sixty years, and through its constant display of idiosyncrasy, its tendency to exaggeration, its pursuit of attenuated elegance, its slight variations on similar themes, its numberless repetitions, acquired a tired sterility which the public came to recognise. Since then 'Mannerist' has been a pejorative term. During the last decades of the century a change was wanted, a new impetus, a virile idea in opposition to the inbred Mannerist derivations. It was at this point that Caravaggio appeared.

Reforms in the Church and their effects on art

The sixteenth century had also seen great changes in the Church in Italy. After the spectacular failure of Savonarola's attack against the wiles of the Borgia Pope, Alexander VI, at the end of the fifteenth century, the Northern Reformation had awakened the Roman Church to activity, and many societies for the reform of the Church were initiated. From the accession of Paul III, the Popes devoted more energy to these reforms than to the arts, and Paul IV and Sixtus V were remarkably active. The Inquisition was revived, the *Index Librarum Prohibitorum* of forbidden books begun and the interest in pagan subject matter in painting discouraged. The classical nude was replaced with clothed figures, and religious subject matter was increasingly in demand; the Council of Trent, in its final session of 1563, had put in its decree that '...by means of stories of the mysteries of our Redemption portrayed by paintings or other representations, the people be instructed and confirmed in the habit of remembering and continually revolving in the mind the articles of faith.'

The Jesuits had introduced the *Spiritual Exercises* of Loyola as a means of emphasising the reality of religious experience and the truths of the Church. They were a practical, down-to-earth road to the spirit and gained large numbers of followers. Their gnostic basis of faith and the resultant return to a realistic approach is reflected in Caravaggio's art. (At the same time it would be unwise to imagine that Caravaggio considered himself an apologist for any part of the Church —Jesuit or not.)

In Rome, where Caravaggio's career properly started about 1590, all the aspects of the changed attitude were reflected, as might be expected. Sixtus V (1585-90), enthusiastic and energetic for reform, aspired to make Rome the most beautiful city in Christendom. He and his successors embarked on large architectural projects which required decoration by painters and sculptors. The most important of these projects was, of course, the rebuilding of St Peter's, which Carlo Maderna was undertaking, converting Michelangelo's central plan into a nave and creating a new façade, but other projects, such as the Pauline Chapel in Santa Maria Maggiore and the Quirinal Palace, were begun.

Unfortunately the artists available were of no great distinction, representing the dying end of Mannerism; the most popular but by no means the most talented was the Cavaliere d'Arpino, whose association with Caravaggio has been noted.

New patrons

The Church was thus the greatest patron of art in Caravaggio's lifetime, as it had been earlier, in the Middle Ages. But it was not the only patron. Private citizens and great churchmen were beginning collections which were not necessarily religious; in fact they showed a wide catholicity of taste. Rome was a wealthy city, becoming the centre of a new devout luxury. Caravaggio was fortunate in finding some of these new patrons interested in his work. Its occasional overt salacity would provide an unacknowledged attraction.

This was the situation in Rome and Italy when Caravaggio came on the scene: a debilitated art of artificial elegance, a great demand for religious painting, a public eager to welcome a virile, stimulating change, and, apparently, only artists of mediocre talent to provide all that was needed. Caravaggio was antipathetic to practically all that surrounded him in art and life. As we have noted from his biographers, he decried the work of other painters, he was intemperate and impatient with what we would now call the Establishment and he would not compromise his sybaritic desires. To be a painter at all he had to be different in his art.

Caravaggio's 'realism'

Different he was, and this difference lay in his acceptance of life, of the reality of hard experience, of the light and shade of events, of the truth of the ordinary visible world and its reference to the truth of religious experience. For him a religious painting was not something to be constructed in a church to fit a given shape and act as a decoration but a humanly lived event which could and should be presented in recognisable relevance to visible experience. Thus he introduced a 'realism' that has always been associated with his name. He was the leader of what came to be known as the *naturalisti* or 'natural' painters.

This return to 'realism' was, however, not his only preoccupation pictorially; in fact, as we shall see later, he was prepared to depart from a strict realism' if he felt occasion demanded. He was an independent servant of the Church providing, in his art, a dramatic interpretation of the vivid truth of the Christian story which the new Roman Church could recognise and which the Protestants welcomed with open arms. As important as his own achievement was the inspiration he gave to others.

To make his 'realist' art more effective he employed means discovered earlier, but not exploited, towards the result he wanted. Most important of these in its far-reaching influence was his use of chiaroscuro. The Englishman, John Elsum, in his *The Art of Painting after the Italian Manner* (1703), describes chiaroscuro with a naïve accuracy: 'Clare-Obscure, is the skill of disposing the Lights and Shadows: These are the two Words united, and instead of saying the Clear and the Obscure, we pronounce them both together, and call them Clare-Obscure in imitation of the Italians, who call it Chiaro-Scuro; and therefore when a Painter gives to his Figures great force and roundness, and sensibly distinguishes the Objects of his Table by Advantageous Lights, followed with great Shadows, we say that this Man understood very well the Art of Clare-Obscure.'

Use of chiaroscuro

Caravaggio did not invent this 'skill' but reintroduced it to produce mystery and drama in his treatment of a subject. This is well illustrated in the *Conversion of St Paul* (Plate 9) and the *Beheading of John the Baptist* (Plate 12). In both of these important paintings light and dark areas are placed in opposition to produce the greatest dramatic effect. When, however, one attempts to determine the source of light a curious fact emerges. There is no consistency—no accurate realism. The main lighting comes from the right in the *Conversion of St Paul*, and it is as well to remember that a strong lateral light may be used to produce a spatially co-ordinated composition. But there is a light which would seem to be in the middle of the picture, for the left arm of St Paul is illuminated from above. When one recalls that there was a 'blinding light' around the scene, it becomes clear that Caravaggio is prepared to subordinate his 'realism' to the dramatic and psychological needs of the subject.

This is true also of his drawing—again the *Conversion* presents a good example. The figure on the ground, the horse, and the old man are all thrust towards the picture plane in an 'unnatural' relationship. The participation of the observer is demanded in this way, but he is not at a natural distance from the scene—the inclination is to step back. This treatment has also necessitated the painter's pushing the figures closer together than 'realism' allows. The far leg of St Paul, the near leg of the old man and the standing foreleg of the horse are in an impossible spatial relationship which any overriding concern for 'realism' could not have accepted.

Treatment of perspective

If we examine the *Martyrdom of St Matthew* (Plate 7) we see that the same is also true of perspective and proportion. The figure of the brutal executioner is deliberately exaggerated in scale for dramatic effectiveness of the scene; the various architectural elements do not fall into a reasonable spatial recession according to standard rules of perspective: the subject is again thrust towards the picture plane and the perspective distorted.

Nevertheless it is not inappropriate to regard Caravaggio as a 'realist' when he is compared with his contemporaries, and his vulgar directness was what they saw to the exclusion of all else. The Florentine-Spanish writer Carducho attacks Caravaggio in these terms: 'Did anyone ever paint, and with as much success, as this monster of genius and talent, almost without rules, without theory, without learning and meditation, solely by the power of his genius and the model in front of him which he simply copied so admirably? I heard a zealot of our profession say that the appearance of this man meant a foreboding of ruin and an end of painting.'

Carducho also regrets that 'most painters follow him as if they were famished,' and it was just this apparent direct 'realism' that they seized upon, particularly the strong chiaroscuric effects, and the spread of his influence in the North was primarily in this aspect. In France, Simon Vouet, Georges de La Tour and the Le Nain brothers were the most important followers, but it was in Holland, that devoutly Protestant country, where his influence was most deeply absorbed and where its inspiration proved most fecund. A number of Dutch painters who worked in Rome were thoroughly imbued with a Caravaggesque spirit and proceeded to affect their compatriots. The most important of these were Honthorst, Terbrugghen and Pieter Lastman. Honthorst had the greatest reputation in his day

Influence in the North

but it is in the influence of Lastman that the real interest lies. It was through him that Rembrandt, his pupil, became acquainted with Caravaggio's art and, deepening and extending it, made it in his own hands a means of human interpretation unrealised by the extrovert Lombard. The distinction is well revealed in a comparison of the treatment of the same subject by Rembrandt and Caravaggio. The Dutch master uses his chiaroscuro to express the same tangibility of darkness as of light and surrounds his gentle figures in a soft radiance which reaches out to the spectator in its sympathetic tenderness. The Italian expresses his delight in the solid volume of the figures in light, but the dark is dead, is negative and forces the interest to the surface of the subject, denying any of the mysterious penetration which Rembrandt achieves.

Another Dutch painter, whom Bernard Berenson describes as 'mysteriously Caravaggesque,' is Vermeer of Delft whose 'realism' is illustrative of the spread of Caravaggio's influence in the North.

In Spain, too, Caravaggio's influence was considerable. Apart from Ribera and Zurbarán, both of whom saw his work in Rome, Velasquez made an early acquaintance with his painting. As we have mentioned before, it is possible that he saw examples of Caravaggio's work when a young painter in Seville through the Prior of the hospital in Rome where Caravaggio stayed during an attack of malaria. In any event, Velasquez visited Rome for the Spanish king Philip IV, and certainly saw Caravaggio's work then. Its effect upon him was different from that upon Rembrandt. He was not concerned with deep chiaroscuro but with the direct tonal 'realism' that he found in Caravaggio's earlier work. The result was an art—not less important than Rembrandt's—which shows a purity and keenness of vision not rivalled in European painting. Through Velasquez' pupil, Murillo, Caravaggio's influence was extended.

Influence in Spain

It is in fact this far-reaching influence—which, through the great masters of the seventeenth century, found its way into the eighteenth and nineteenth centuries—that perhaps constitutes the larger portion of Caravaggio's importance.

Caravaggio's importance assessed

His independent, anti-cultural attitude freed Italian art from subservience to the sterility of the Mannerists and breathed the fresh air of direct experience into musty interiors and minds. It was an art which invited expansion, and thus, through a multitude of followers, this dedicated Bohemian became one of the most potent forces in the history of European art.

Plate 2 *1592 Oil on canvas 26×20¹/₂ inches Borghese Gallery, Rome*

Boy with Fruit (Bacchino Malato)

This work has at various times been ascribed to other painters but
is now generally acknowledged to be by Caravaggio and is identified
with the painting sequestered by the tax authorities from the
studio of the Cavaliere d'Arpino in 1607, and described as
a 'youth with a wreath of ivy around his head and a bunch of grapes
in his hand.' This ties it up with the picture described by Baglione
as 'Bacchus with some grapes of various sorts, done very diligently,
but rather drily,' and as 'the first of the small pictures painted
by him in a mirror,' after he left the studio of the Cavaliere d'Arpino.
Since Caravaggio is supposed to have been set by d'Arpino to
paint 'fruit and flowers,' this may have been an extra exercise that
he gave himself to include a figure. The use of a mirror
suggests a possible self-portrait, and several authorities have
connected this with Caravaggio's convalescence from malaria in the
Hospital for the Poor in Santa Maria della Consolazione and believe it to have
been done at this time. The wan lips and tired eyes certainly
do not indicate good health, and this is not necessarily a Bacchus since
the usual vine-wreath is replaced by ivy in the hair and there is no wine.
The characteristic 'forward' treatment of the figure and table
brings the painting out at the viewer, and there are some of
the weaknesses of the *Bacchus* repeated here. The sash does not rest
happily on the table; the leg is not convincingly placed;
in fact, the perspective is generally unconvincing.
The painting was among those given by Pope Paul V to
Cardinal Scipione Borghese, one of the greatest collectors
and patrons of the age, whose collection forms the basis of
the Borghese Gallery in Rome.

Plate 3   *1592   Oil on canvas   27¹/₂×26¹/₂ inches   Borghese Gallery, Rome*

Boy with a Basket of Fruit

Like the previous plate, this painting was in the Cavaliere
d'Arpino's effects which were sequestered by the tax authorities
and which passed into the collection of Cardinal Scipione Borghese.
Although this painting, too, has been attributed to other artists, it
is now generally ascribed to Caravaggio and dates from the period
of his apprenticeship to d'Arpino.

The concentration of interest on the basket of fruit, so very
similar to the Ambrosiana still-life (Plate 5), distracts attention
from the rather weak head and shoulders which the earlier work
of Caravaggio frequently shows.   The head itself, it is suggested
by Friedlaender, may have been done by someone else in the studio of
d'Arpino and has, certainly, a rather sweetly effeminate character
reminiscent more of Murillo than Caravaggio.

One might mention here something that occurs again and again in
Caravaggio's *œuvre*.   The basket of fruit, if traced to its full
circular extent, does not leave room for the chest of the youth holding it;
he would appear to be concave, and this inconsistency tends to diminish
the conviction of the painting.   This is true also of the far
shoulder, which seems to cut into the background.   Perhaps the
most notable example of this tendency in Caravaggio's work can be seen
in Plate 9 and is discussed in the notes.

Plate 4   c. 1595   Oil on canvas   41³/₄ × 38¹/₄ inches   Doria Pamphili Gallery, Rome

The Repentant Magdalene

This painting is described by Bellori in some detail as illustrative
of Caravaggio's ability in 'naturalism'.   He says he is able
'to imitate the hues of nature with a few colours,' and that '...he
painted a young girl seated on a chair and passed her off as a Magdalene.'
In his use of the ordinary model for religious figures, Caravaggio made
no concessions to what might be called the elevated spirit
of the subject matter; in this he differed from his contemporaries.
The 'genre' nature of the painting here is emphasised by the jewels
in casual disarray on the floor and the common bare interior
as well as by the simple treatment of the figure.   One can really
feel that the title of the Magdalene was an afterthought.
The spatial treatment here is more conventional than in the previous
examples, and there does seem to be an attempt to relate the large
dark shape above to the contrite, isolated figure of the young girl.
With all these criticisms, however, it should be remembered that this
is the work of a man barely twenty.

Plate 5   *1596*   *Oil on canvas*   *18×25¹/₄ inches*   *Ambrosiana Gallery, Milan*

Basket of Fruit

This is a unique work in Caravaggio's surviving *œuvre*.
It is the still-life attributed to him, and it certainly does not
date from the period of his apprenticeship to d'Arpino.
It is of a kind not then fashionable—in fact Bellori claims
that Caravaggio started the fashion for such works, which, if true,
surely suggests numerous examples which have not survived.
There is some belief that this painting was originally not a still-life
but was part of a larger composition.   Although a recent x-ray
of this painting revealed nothing of importance behind the warm cream
background, it is probable that this background was added later
(to cover a defect and lay emphasis on the fruit?), since the cream
colour overlaps the leaves in several places.   Again it might
be noted that the twig on the right does not come from the basket but
seems to have spilled over from some larger container not included.
This tends to suggest that the painting may have been cut down.
But any dismemberment must have taken place very early,
since this is the painting mentioned in a codicil of a
gift to the Accademia Ambrosiana by Archbishop Borromeo, in 1607.
The painting is close in character to the basket of fruit in
the *Supper at Emmaus* in the National Gallery, London, even to the
extent of the low perspective viewpoint, which, incidentally, is
inaccurate in the *Emmaus*.   Although not a direct study for the *Emmaus*,
it is near enough to be dated with some certainty as 1596.
Caravaggio's constant concern with the actual appearance of
things has led him to include the blemishes with the perfections.
The beautiful red apple, the one that immediately attracts,
is seen to contain the worm hole that repels, and in the rich
luxuriousness lies one withered leaf which betokens the decay of all.

Plate 6 *c. 1600 Oil on canvas 10³/₄×8¹/₈ feet Contarelli Chapel, Church of San Luigi dei Francesi, Rome*

The Calling of St Matthew (detail)

The commission for the paintings in the Contarelli Chapel has been
discussed in the introduction, and it has been indicated that
the dating of these paintings is extremely difficult.
It seems most likely that they were completed by 1599, when the
chapel was opened, but it is possible that Caravaggio
still had work to finish on them. It is known that they
were not finally fixed to the wall until December, 1600.
The detail illustrated here is from the right-side lateral
painting—the call to St Matthew to join Christ;
Plate 7, the left lateral, depicts the martyrdom of St Matthew.
The altar-piece itself was also painted by Caravaggio and depicts
St Matthew and the Angel.
As described by Bellori, 'Christ is calling St Matthew to the
Apostolate, in which several heads are portrayed in a natural manner,
among them the saint, who, interrupting his counting of money,
turns to the Lord, his hand on his breast. Nearby an old man puts
his spectacles on his nose and looks at the youth at the corner of
the table who is drawing all the money to himself.'
The detail illustrated depicts the two youths nearest to Christ
who have been disturbed by His arrival. They are dressed in
foppish clothing, not at all typical of the day. The 'naturalism'
with which Caravaggio has been associated did not prevent his use of
artificial props, and in fact, as is indicated in the introduction,
his 'realism' is of a formal kind.

Plate 7   c. 1601-3   Oil on canvas $10^3/_4 \times 11^1/_2$ feet   Contarelli Chapel, Church of San Luigi dei Francesi, Rome

The Martyrdom of St Matthew (detail)

St Matthew is supposed to have been slain in Ethiopia at the
orders of Hirtacus, the King, but this story is not universally accepted.
Caravaggio had great difficulty with this painting, and there
are two earlier versions under the present one on the canvas which
have recently been revealed by radiographs. The scale of
the figures, their disposition and their number varies in each
version, and although it is not possible to discover from them the
development of Caravaggio's thought, it seems clear that he
greatly increased the drama—not to say melodrama—in the
final painting. Most of the figures have been moved and the central
group altered entirely. The result is something of a pictorial mess;
the scale is inconsistent and the spatial relationships are impossible.
Nevertheless the work is immensely impressive, since, as with
all the greatest art, it implies and suggests more than it depicts.
The detail shown here embraces most of the action of the
painting. The fallen saint is threatened by a towering, shouting
near-naked giant, the very epitome of brute mercenary force,
while a terrified youth, too frightened to run yet unable to turn away
from the scene of horror, screams in sympathy.
The foreground figure, also nearly naked, emphasises, in a parallel and
reverse movement to the giant, the impossibility of escape of the
wounded martyr on the ground. Above, indicating the divine
interest, an angel stretches down from a thick, billowy cloud
to receive the martyr's soul. On the left, one can just see the
small group of helpless onlookers, among whom is Caravaggio himself.
This is a scene of despair and is in keeping with
Caravaggio's insistence upon human inadequacy and imperfection.

Plate 8   *1598   Oil on canvas   60¹/₂×43¹/₄ inches   Kaiser Friedrich Museum, Berlin*

Cupid Victorious

Painted for the great collector and patron of Caravaggio, the
Marchese Vincenzo Giustiniani, this is a remarkable *tour de force*
designed to excite the sensibilities of the influential connoisseur.
The young boy, seductively posed and far from innocent,
is painted with a direct salacious interest and all the adjuncts
emphasise the physical attractiveness of the young flesh;
the hard forms of the musical instruments, the soft drapings of what
appears to be a bed, the convincing wings, for once seeming to be a
real part of the figure, and the metal cuirass showing the soldiers
susceptibilities, all work to that end.
It is a marvellous example of the power that Caravaggio had of
transforming the obviously vulgar—could the face belong to
any other than a Neapolitan *scugnizzi?*—into an image of rare
imagination and varied implication.
For once the space is consistently handled, and the deep chiaroscuro is
designed to add to the mysterious invitation of an ambiguous love.
This is a mischievous and sophisticated work.

Plate 9   *1601*   *Oil on canvas* $7^1/_2 \times 5^3/_4$ *feet*   *Church of Santa Maria del Popolo, Rome*

The Conversion of St Paul

Tiberio Cerasi acquired in July, 1600, a chapel in Santa Maria del
Popolo and commissioned Caravaggio to provide two paintings for it.
These were the *Crucifixion of St Peter* and the *Conversion of St Paul*,
and Caravaggio agreed to supply preliminary sketches and to paint
the final works on cypress panels.   His first panels were refused
as being unsatisfactory and they were acquired by Cardinal Sannesio.
The second versions, which may have been commissioned by
Caravaggio's patron the Marchese Giustiniani since Cerasi
had died in the interval, are those that are still in place.
This version of the subject is most unusual and indicates the
independent spirit with which Caravaggio approached it.
The great horse is the dominant feature of the painting, representing
perhaps the uncomprehending brute world which cannot see or feel
the glorious impact of the spirit of Grace, while Saul himself lies
helpless and obviously sightless on the ground.   Even the old man
holding the horse does not realise the importance of the event.
Venturi has well described the work: '... here the light has
its own spiritual language, it constitutes the magic circle into which
Saul has entered, and the body of the horse is nothing but
an excuse for a luminous mass which embraces the sinner.'
The forcing of the action towards the picture plane and the necessity
for the vast size of the horse has led Caravaggio into those
inconsistencies of space which have been noted before.
There is no real room for the far leg of Saul, the ground does not
recede sufficiently to allow for the relative positions
of the horse and the body of Saul, and the old man's body cannot be
correctly related to his legs.   Nevertheless these things
are not noted at first, the immediate effect being one of intimacy
and reality, of religious power and of pictorial originality.

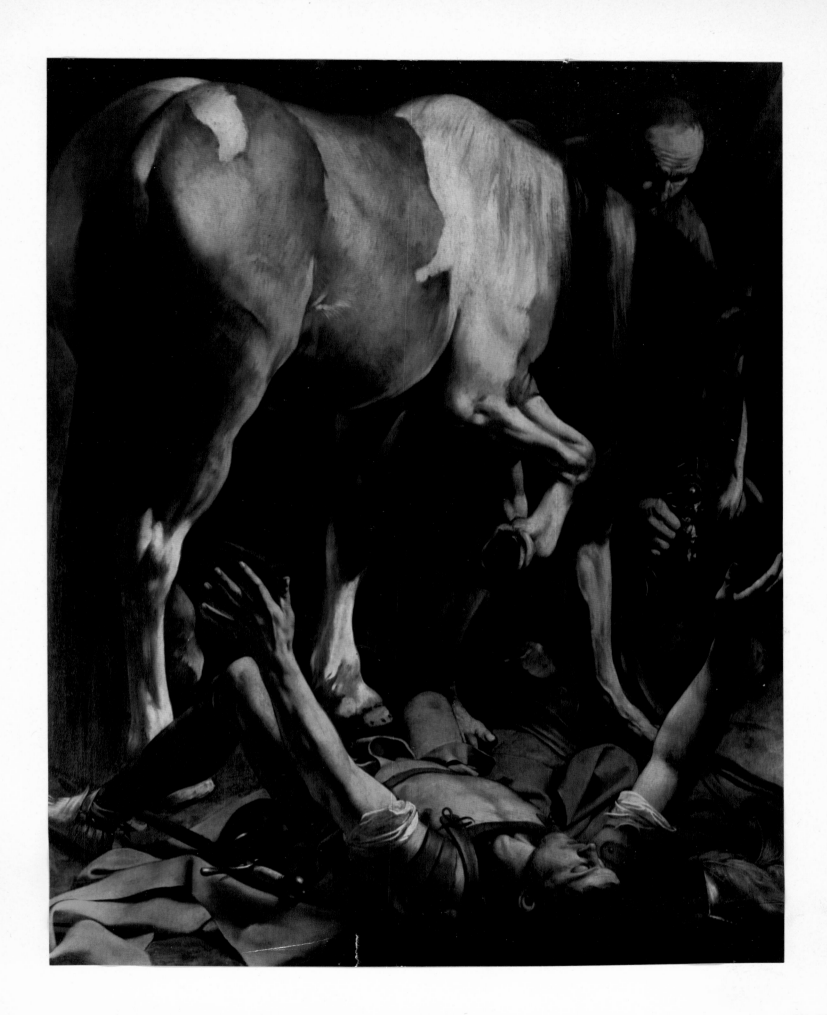

Plate 10   *1606   Oil on canvas 57×77 inches   Brera, Milan*

The Supper at Emmaus (detail)

The Supper at Emmaus was a popular subject. The two disciples
Cleophas and Peter Simon had invited the unknown Pilgrim to take
supper with them, and only when He blessed and broke the bread was
His real identity known to them. It was a moment of wonder and revelation.
Caravaggio painted two versions of this dramatic subject: one is in
the National Gallery, London; the other, of which the centre detail is
illustrated here, is in the Brera Gallery, having been purchased from
the Patrizi family for whom it was painted during Caravaggio's flight
from Rome after his banishment. It is a more mature version than the
earlier and shows that the scene does not demand theatrics.
The National Gallery version shows the figures in highly
stylized expressions of surprise and seems to be mainly an
exercise in chiaroscuro, drawing and dramatic expression.
The Brera version is quieter and more restrained, the light is
more sympathetically handled and the drawing of Christ (shown here)
more reasonable and effective. Even so both of them reveal the
exuberant vulgarity of Caravaggio's mind when compared with
the Louvre painting of the same subject by Rembrandt,
the human depth of which makes the Caravaggios appear 'flashy'.
As usual, the drawing of the still-life in the painting is
executed with care and in the Brera version with more accurate perspective.

Plate 11   *1605   Oil on canvas   49×39³/₄ inches   Borghese Gallery, Rome*

David with the head of Goliath

Caravaggio painted this work for Cardinal Scipione Borghese—thus its
presence in the Borghese Gallery. The head of Goliath is said
to be a self-portrait, and it does in fact greatly resemble
the known self-portrait in the *Martyrdom of St Matthew*—it is
typical of the harsh determined features of Caravaggio
as he is described by those who knew him. In portraying himself
thus as Goliath he may have been intending to suggest that,
although of great strength, he is the victim of innocent
confidence with all the implications that the picture conveys, in the
soft tenderness of the young David as he looks on his handiwork.
The greatly overscale head of Goliath is the most important
feature of the painting and serves, in its coarseness, to suggest the
wages of experience.

Plate 12   *1608   Oil on canvas   11⁷/₈ × 17¹/₈ feet   Cathedral of St John, Valletta, Malta*

The Beheading of John the Baptist

This is the most important work that Caravaggio executed
while in Malta, and it was well received by the Grand Master.
Bellori in his biography described the painting with vivid accuracy:
'For the Church of St John he (the Grand Master Alof de Wignacourt)
made him paint the decollation of the Saint, fallen to the ground;
while the headsman, as though he had not already dealt him
a sword blow, drew his knife and grasped his hair to sever his head
from his shoulders. Herodias' daughter gazes intently and
an old woman stands aghast at the spectacle, while the prison warder,
in Turkish dress, points at the dreadful deed. In this work
Caravaggio exerted his skill to the utmost, with such daring
that the priming of the canvas serves for the middle tones:
in such wise that the Grand Master gave him, besides the Cross,
a rich collar of gold about his neck, and two slaves,
with other marks of esteem and appreciation of his work.'
The dramatic effect of the composition, in which the semi-circle
of figures, centred hermetically upon the dreadful deed,
is balanced by the isolated overlookers in a high window,
is remarkably powerful. Caravaggio here has mastered the use of
empty space in pictorial drama and does not again quite return
to the same power. There is an ease and assurance which probably
owes a lot to the apparent settled favour of the Grand Master.
The fact that, soon after, he became a fugitive for the rest
of his life doubtless contributed to his inability to rise again to
the same stature.

Published by

BATCHWORTH PRESS LIMITED

Spring House • Spring Place • London NW 5

by arrangement with

Istituto Geografico De Agostini S.p.A. • Novara, Italy

Text © Books for Pleasure Ltd., 1961

Printed in Italy